The Dance

The Dance

Lyrics by Tony Arata

A Round Stone Press Book

NEW YORK

Photography Credits
Photograph copyrights are held by the parties listed below.

THE IMAGE BANK

Page 5: Gary Bistram; Page 7: Fernando Bueno; Page 9: Sandy King;
Page 11: Hans Wendler; Page 17: Steve Dunwell; Page 19: Dann Coffey;
Page 27: Michael Melford; Page 31: Tim Bieber; Page 33: Bullaty/Lomeo;
Pages 42-43: P. M. De Renzis; Page 45: Sobel/Klonsky

FPG INTERNATIONAL

Page 13: John Terence Turner; Page 15: Terry Qing;
Pages 20-21: Larry West; Page 23: Michael Kornafel;
Page 25: Dave Bartruff; Page 29: Carmona Photog.;
Page 35: Richard Laird; Page 37: Jerry Sieve;
Page 39: Willinger; Page 47: Mike Valeri

Page 41: Courtesy of Fran Kapp Photography

A ROUND STONE PRESS BOOK
Directors: Marsha Melnick, Susan E. Meyer, Paul Fargis
Developmental Editor: Thomas G. Fiffer
Design: Harakawa Sisco Inc

Library of Congress Cataloging-in-Publication Data
Arata, Tony.
  [Dance. Text]
  The dance / lyrics by Tony Arata. —1st ed.
     p.   cm.
  "A Round Stone Press book."
  ISBN 1-56282-746-4
  1. Country music—Texts.   I. Title.
ML54.6.A7D3   1993 <Case>
782.42'1642'0268—dc20   93-24900

FIRST EDITION

10 9 8 7 6 5 4 3 2 1

*Looking back
on the
memory of*

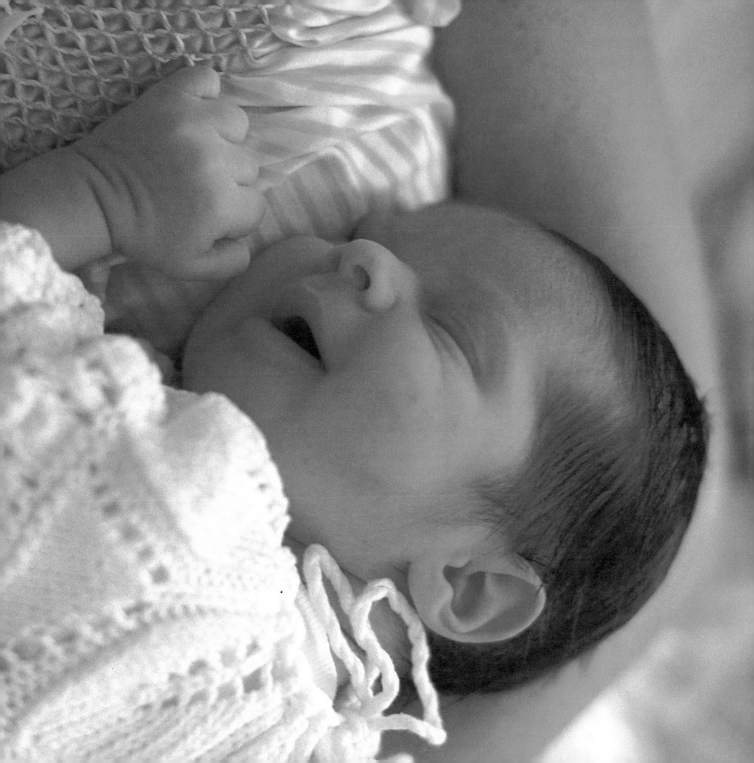

The dance we shared

'neath the stars above

For a moment
all the world was right

How could I have known

that you'd ever say goodbye

And now I'm glad
I didn't know

The way it all would end,
the way it all would go

Our lives
are better left
to chance,

I could have missed the pain

But I'd've had to miss the dance

Holding you
I held everything

For a moment
wasn't I a king

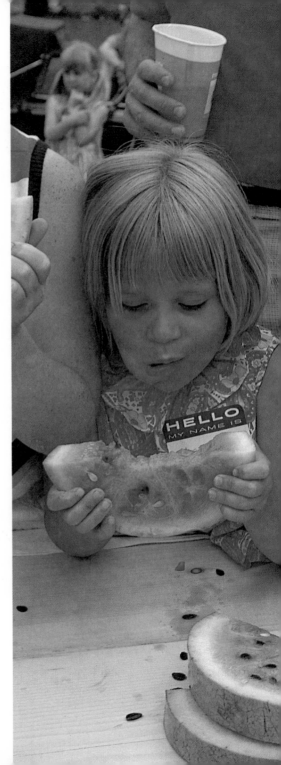

But if I'd only known

How the king would fall

*Hey who's to say
you know*

I might have chanced it all

Yes my life is better left to chance

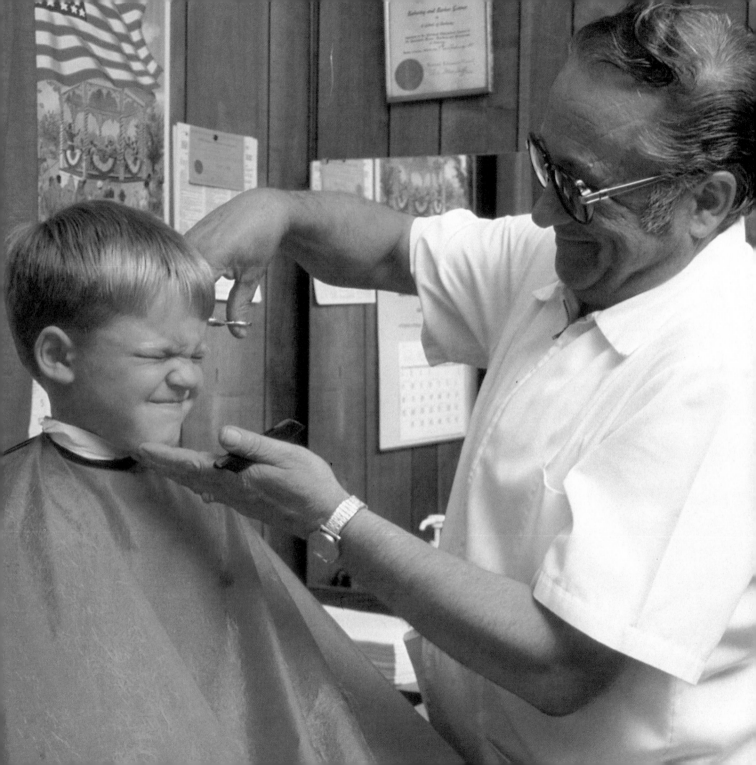

*I could have missed
the pain*

*but I'd've had to miss
the dance*

The Dance

TONY ARATA

Looking back on the memory of
The dance we shared 'neath the stars above
For a moment all the world was right
How could I have known that you'd ever say goodbye

And now I'm glad I didn't know
The way it all would end, the way it all would go
Our lives are better left to chance, I could have missed the pain
But I'd've had to miss the dance

Holding you I held everything
For a moment wasn't I a king
But if I'd only known how the king would fall
Hey who's to say you know I might have chanced it all

Yes, my life is better left to chance
I could have missed the pain but I'd've had to miss the dance